India

By KALIM WINATA and REED DARMON

CHRONICLE BOOKS
SAN FRANCISCO

Library of Congress Cataloging-in-Publication Data:
Winata, Kalim.
    Made in India / by Kalim Winata and Reed Darmon.
      p. cm.
    ISBN: 978-0-8118-6502-9
    1. Commercial art—India. 2. Graphic arts—India. I. Darmon, Reed. II. Title.

NC998.6.I5W56 2008
741.60954'09045–dc22
                                    2008010672

Manufactured in China

Designed by Reed Darmon

Consultation and translations by Sandip Roy and Ravi Nayar.
Translations by Ravi Jagannadhan and Dr. Kalavathy Ravindran.

Photography is by Alan Borrud, Portland, Oregon, Reed Darmon,
Portland, Oregon, and Harlim Djauhar Winata/Glam:fab, Hong Kong.

10 9 8 7 6 5 4 3 2 1

Chronicle Books LLC
680 Second Street
San Francisco, California 94107
www.chroniclebooks.com

PAGE 1: Ganesh, the elephant-headed god, is known as the remover of obstacles.

PREVIOUS SPREAD: Detail from a devotional poster showing Krishna revealing his true
manifestation, called Visvarupa (all gods in one), to the warrior prince Arjuna, in a scene from
the Bhagavad-Gita, the philosophical heart of the epic story the Mahabharata.

OPPOSITE: The personification "Mother India," which first appeared during the independence
movement against England, is shown on a matchbox cover.

To my mother, Jenni
— Kalim Winata

To my mother, Beatrice
— Reed Darmon

Introduction

Experiencing the popular visual culture of India is like tasting Navratan Korma, a delicious northern Indian curry dish. The spices get your attention, and the varied colors and textures of the other ingredients stimulate and delight all the senses.

From folk art and religious iconography to Bollywood posters and household product packaging, vintage Indian design, like the subcontinent's cuisine, is rich, colorful, and diverse. Today, as in the past, the streets of India are vibrant with signs in saturated colors. Women stroll in saris of flamboyant hues and intricate patterns. Shops are filled with packages that compete like dancing peacocks for customers' attention.

India's colorful aesthetic, with its long lineage in the realms of worship and personal adornment, found new forms of expression in the early twentieth century. Fabric labels and packaging of goods from England picked up motifs from the great tradition of Indian miniature painting in order to appeal to Indian national tastes. The floral patterns, geometric designs, and intricate manuscript borders that were widespread during India's sixteenth- through nineteenth-century Mughal Empire became the vocabulary of commercial art. Scenes of court life, tableaux from Hindu mythology, and portraits of maharajas (great kings), gods, and goddesses were common in advertisement, their graphic style mimicking the Rajput school of painting that flourished in Hindu-ruled Rajasthan. Soon Indian-made products began using motifs of royalty and religion on their labels to sell *beedis* (Indian-style cigarettes), *paan masala* (chewing tobacco), household goods, books, firecrackers, and cosmetics. Incense labels featured

VIDYUT METALLICS

female figures, either suggestive pinups or chaste, angelic attendants to the gods — the same beauties who have welcomed devotees to the path of ecstasy and worship for a thousand years.

In India, the culture's beloved gods and goddesses truly live among mortals, dwelling in effigy in shrines, temples, shops, and homes. Attending a devotional festival at the vast Shrinathji Temple in Rajasthan, such as the one marking the full moon after Diwali, can have the feel of going to a sports event or even a rock concert in the West. Crowds anxiously queue up past the v.i.p. section to meet their favorite deity. Mantras are shouted from one corner to the other in giant waves of sound.

Like their ancient Greek counterparts, Indian gods and goddesses possess human emotions, and their legends are stories of triumphs and tragedies. Shiva, father of the god Ganesh, cutting off his son's head and replacing it with that of an elephant. Sita's husband questioning her honor after her kidnap by Ravana. Images from these stories are seen everywhere, and this ubiquity may be credited in large part to one man, Raja Ravi Varma. As a painter, he achieved a breakthrough synthesis of European form and Indian themes, employing European neoclassical and romantic styles to create a new look for the traditional Hindu gods. Wildly popular among European as well as Indian elites, Ravi Varma was also dedicated to spreading an

New Look
SAREES

**LOVELINESS IN
EVERY LINE**

☆

U.N. PURSRAM

SILKS ★ SAREES ★ UNDERWEAR

Hornby Road — BOMBAY

appreciation of art to the masses. In 1894, he founded a printing press to make these images accessible to the populace in the form of affordable reproductions. With the use of shadows, depth, and theatrical poses, he made subjects from Indian epics such as the Mahabharata and the Ramayana imaginable to consumers in a fresh way. The god Brahma, for example, floating on his lotus blossom just after springing into existence fully formed, is portrayed for the public with unprecedented realism.

Ravi Varma Press and other print shops such as Chitrashala Press and S.S. Brijbasi & Sons brought lithograph and oleograph prints to new heights in quality and distribution. Celebrating gods, maharajas, native beauties, and national heroes, the prints played a role in arousing Indian identity during the colonial period.

But the most brilliant strain of India's graphic culture is its cinema — not only Bollywood (its name a conflation of Hollywood and Bombay) but Kollywood (from the Kodambakkam area of Tamil Nadu state) and numerous other regional studios producing films in the Bengali, Kannada, Malayalam, and Telugu languages. In India, film has exploded the isolation of rural from urban and of the entire subcontinent from the rest of the world. By 1960, for a few rupees an Indian worker could be transported to the magnificent Palace of Mirrors in a forbidden land via the movie *Mughal-e-Azam* (The Great Mughal). On the soundtrack of a typical Bollywood movie, sitar strings and tabla drumbeats mix with Western-style show tunes, rock, jazz, and electronica; female dancers in nose rings and skin-tight beaded outfits gyrate with god-like males to music with moves ranging from Punjabi Bhangra to Fred Astaire, Elvis Presley, and Justin Timberlake. The power of cinema over Indian audiences has also resulted in surreal meldings of pop culture, politics, and religion: The Bollywood star is treated as a sort of demigod; the 1975 film *Jai Santoshi Maa* (Hail to the Mother Santoshi) actually elevated a figure in local folk legend to a widely worshipped Hindu goddess; popular Kollywood star M.G. Ramchandran became a beloved populist politician. Over time, movies influenced the other arts, and even religious prints often acquired a cinematic, "filmie" feel.

Devotional prints have evolved with the times, and it is interesting to compare the early examples in the front of this book with treatments of the same subjects in the back. By the middle of the twentieth century, European naturalism, with its earth-toned and curiously un-Indian landscapes, gave way to elaborate schematic designs, radiant colors, and figures in straight-ahead poses, holding intense eye contact with the viewer. It was as if the devotional image had reasserted its use as a totemic object or focal point for the act of worship. And it was this graphic style — truly original, popular, and distinctly Indian — that struck non-Indians as psychedelic when the prints became popular in the West in the 1960s.

The ephemera presented here offer a survey of popular Indian graphics from a Western perspective. In no way conclusive or complete, the collection serves as a modest exploration, appreciation, and admiration of a culture that has not lost sight of the divine in the world around it. — KALIM WINATA

Ads shown in the introduction are from the October 1951 issue of *Film India* magazine.

10

Paintings on mica were produced mainly for the tourist market in the late nineteenth and early twentieth centuries. The subject matter ranged from deities to daily life. Queen Mary was presented with a set of mica paintings during her visit in 1911.

∧ This mica painting depicts the devotional practice of *pooja* (worship) of Kali, goddess of time.

< A genre scene of an acrobatic street performer, painted on mica.

^ A hand-painted card of a single head provides the face for other cards showing costumes from various regions of India, on this novelty item from the beginning of the twentieth century.

> A genre painting in gouache on paper for the tourist market depicting a noble-woman and her dog.

India's great tradition of miniature paintings, portraying religious tales and scenes of courtly life, was cleverly appropriated into commercial design in the beginning of the twentieth century.

> The Begum of Bhopal, on a label for the Wole Satchi Company.

^ A label on a package of thread produced for Ishwarlal J. Jariwala & Co.

> Hayashiras, a horse-headed form of Vishnu symbolizing energy and knowledge, on an imported product label by Kaloomal Shorimal.

∧ An acrobatic act on a fabric label from Chika Ltd.

Kaloomull Shorimull Importers AMRITSAR

TRADE MARK

1lb NETT   CARTHAMINE   When Packed

Packed in Bombay.

^ Court life featuring a maharaja and his courtesan on a label for Kaloomull Shorimull fabrics.

^ The five-headed form of Shiva on a label for Nathumal Shorimal fabrics.

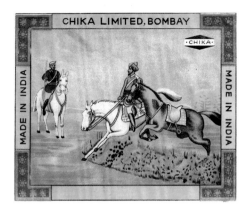

< A fabric label showing a maharaja and his beloved horses for Chika Limited.

< A portrait of a maharaja for Nathumal Shorimal Importers.

> This early and ornate label, with the goddess Saraswati as its central figure, was made by the F. Steiner Co. for the Indian market.

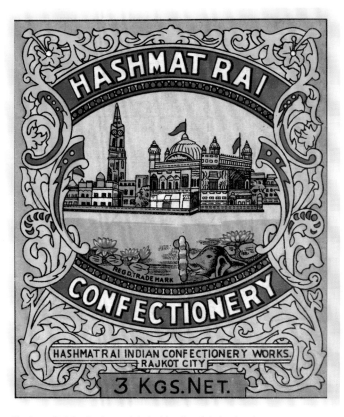

^ Hashmat Rai Confectionery label with a floral design border
that recalls Mughal paintings and manuscripts.

> "Best Turkey Red", a fabric label
for William Stirling & Sons,
in the style of Rajput paintings.

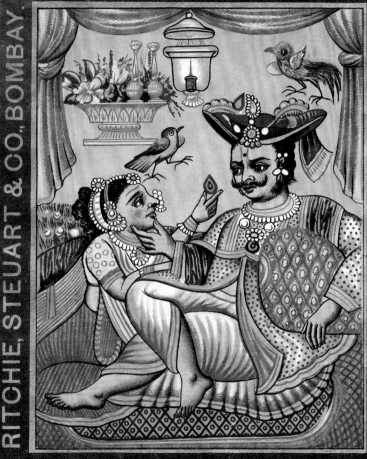

WILLIAM STIRLING & SONS,

RITCHIE, STEUART & CO., BOMBAY.

No. BEST TURKEY RED. Yds.

∧ A lithograph print from 1937 of the national hero Rana Pratap Singh of Mewar, a region surrounding Udaipur in southern Rajasthan, printed by Modern Litho Works, Bombay.

> This fabric label depicts a beauty whose eyes are reminiscent of a style of festive folk painting called Kalighat.

^ The introduction of Western printing techniques, such as lithography and oleography, created a market not only for devotional prints but also for images of rajas and other political figures. Above is an old print of the Maharaja of Gwalior.

< A print entitled "Hindoostan Maharajas" by Ravi Varma Press.

BOURNE & SHEPHERD पटियाला SIMLA

^ This *carte de visite,* portraying the
Maharaja of Patialla, was taken
by Bourne & Shepherd, Simla.

^ A *carte de visite* depicting an unknown bejewelled courtesan, by F. Nelson, "Traveling Photographer."

‹ An albumen photograph showing an unknown nobleman in a fine silk shirt.

˅ Christmas greeting card from the Maharaja of Kolhapur,
a city currently located in the state of Marashtra, also showing
the region's British administrator, Sir Frederick Sykes.

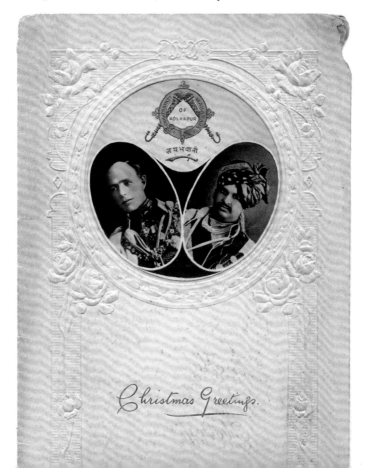

Christmas Greetings.

An example of extraordinarily ornate printing, including gold ink, on a chromolithograph showing the god Vishnu and his consort Laxmi.

All the gods and goddesses of Hinduism originated from one manifestation called Murti. Of these, the three major gods are Brahma, the creator; Vishnu, the preserver; and Shiva, the destroyer.

^ The god Brahma, on the lotus blossom, is "self-born" from the navel of Vishnu in this print published by Ravi Varma Press.

> Shiva, lord of dance, destruction, and renewal, dances to the rhythm of the universe while stepping on the demon Apasmara, the symbol of ignorance, in this print published by the Ravi Udaya Vijaya Offset Litho company.

Two ancient epic stories, the Ramayana and the Mahabharata, have been a limitless sources of imagery for devotional prints, calendars, and even advertising since the beginning of Indian graphic arts.

∧ These colorful letterforms for the word "Ram" contain four of the main characters in the Ramayana.

> Krishna reveals his true manifestation, called Visvarupa (all gods in one), to the warrior prince Arjuna in a scene from the Bhagavad-Gita, the philosophical heart of the epic story the Mahabharata.

^ The Ramayana, a tale of righteousness and loyalty, is a story about a dutiful husband, Ram, rescuing his wife, Sita, from the demon Ravana. In the print above, Ram and Sita celebrate returning to their rightful throne in Ayodhia.

< In this scene from the Ramayana, the villain king Ravana sits on his throne resting on the nine planets, which are represented by nine kinglike figures.

∧ In this print entitled "The Meeting of Vishnu and Shiva," the super-
imposed heads of the elephant and the cow symbolize the harmony
that exists between the two Hindu sects that these animals represent.

< Scenes such as these from the the tales of the Ramayana
are widely performed as devotional plays, called Ram Lila,
in northern India during the festival of Dussehra.

^ The powerful character Bhima, who possesses the strength of one hundred elephants and carries an iron mace, is famous for defeating the mighty King Shalya in the epic tale the Mahabharata.

^ Indians have personified the planets as gods and goddesses in a manner similar to the Greeks. Here the celestial deity Shani Deva represents the planet Saturn.

^ The tribulations of Damayanti reach a terrible
point in this scene from "The Book of the Forest,"
one of the stories in the Mahabharata.

> "The Birth of Shakuntala" depicts the celibate
sage Vishvamitra being shown the shameful
results of his seduction by the nymph Menake.

Karma, the accumulated effect of a person's actions, is an important concept in Hinduism, as well as in Jainism and Buddhism.

< ^ These two prints entitled "Naraka" (Hell) depict various unrighteous acts in Indian culture, and their associated punishments.

45

∧ This image of Swami Dayanand (1824–1883), founder of Arya Samaj, a Hindu reform movement, was painted by an artist from Chitrashala Press in Dehradun.

< Mahavira, the twenty-fourth enlightened teacher and saint of Jainism, achieved spiritual freedom by resisting all manner of worldly temptations and surviving torture by fire.

Printmakers provided for the Indian Islamic market with
these pictures of calligraphic phrases in praise of Allah.

الله انصر من نصر دين محمد الأمين وخذل من خذل دين محمد

49

> During Holi, the Festival of Colors, powder and water of different hues are thrown at celebrants to welcome the beginning of spring. This courtly version of the festival, entitled "Ranpanchmi," was printed by Shree Vasudeo Picture Co., Bombay.

^ In this curious print, the wives of Kaliya,
the poisonous serpent-king, plead with Krishna
to spare their snake-husband's life.

> This print of Mami Wata, the water goddess of Africa who
charms the snake-gods, originated as an image painted by a German
painter in 1928. Prints of the image, made in Mumbai, India, became
a crosscultural phenomenon when they were circulated in Ghana,
Africa, and went on to popularize her cult in central Africa.

The artists of S.S. Brijbasi Press, one of India's most prolific printmakers, adopted a romantic, European style of landscape painting from the signature style of Nathadwara artists in Rajasthan. The print above, of Bradjakishor, the young Krishna, painted by Narottam Narain, and the print at left, "Lord Shiva Meditating on Mt. Kailash," were both from S.S. Brijbasi Press.

^ Garuda stretches his wings to carry Lord Vishnu and his consorts, in this popular print by Ravi Varma Press.

> The evil King Hiranyakashipu, who could not be destroyed by "man or beast," "day or night," or "inside or outside," is here destroyed by Narasimha, the lion-headed incarnation of Vishnu, half-man, at twilight, in a doorway.

Krishna, the eighth reincarnation of Vishnu, is normally associated with love and devotion. Radha, his most famous paramour, is often standing at his side, as seen in these two versions. The print on the left is a more traditional Indian approach and has been accentuated with glitter.

^ The playful Krishna teases the bathing cowherd girls by hiding their clothes in a tree, in this early and relatively modest version of the famous scene.

< Krishna means "the dark one" and he is usually depicted as having dark blue skin.

An early lithograph print entitled "Tukaram Ji" shows a revered seventeenth-century Marathi poet ascending to heaven.

As in the Victorian era in the West, eroticism in India was veiled in mythology and devotion, and the models were legitimized as goddesses, nymphs, and historical heroines. The print above is a scene from the tale of "Shantanu Matsacandha," a love story between King Shantanu and the ferryboat maiden Satyavati.

^ A Ravi Varma Press beauty entitled "Parsi Woman."

< This print, published by Ravi Varma Press and entitled "Bathing," has the jewelry, hair ornaments, and garment seams accented with copper repoussé sequins, a popular treatment for prints in the early twentieth century.

> This print entitled "Gopi Garhani" (The Cowherd Housewives) depicts a group of women come to complain to Yoshoda, young Krishna's foster mother, that he has stolen their butter and yogurt, and broken the pots as well. His actions are actually a metaphor for stealing their hearts. The print is from the Calendar Mfg. Co.

∧ Krishna, the cowherd, uses his magic flute to enchant all the creatures on earth, in a print whose fine printing highlights an extraordinary headdress.

< An early twentieth-century lithograph of Krishna enchanting earth's creatures by Ravi Varma Press.

Krishna is worshipped widely throughout all parts of India, and the iconography of his representation has evolved into many different and curious forms according to local tastes and customs.

∧ Here, Krishna (black faced) is portrayed as Jagannath, the Lord of the World, standing alongside his siblings at a temple in Orissa, in a print by Modern Litho Works, Bombay.

> This print depicts Krishna as the incarnation Shri Natji, in a style that can be found in Nathadwara, Rajasthan.

^ A charming genre scene called "Mother and Child,"
printed by the Chitrashala Press, circa 1880.

< Krishna is depicted as a god-child enjoying an Indian sweet called *laddu*.

^ In this story, Krishna as Ranchod Ji forsakes war by taking up
residency in the town of Dwaraka, Gujarat, in what this artist
imagines is an ornate palace.

< Vishnu and his twenty-four avators (incarnations), by Ravi Varma Press.

∧ The rich tradition of Indian self-adornment is displayed in this bejewelled image of Shri Ram Chandra Ji, one of Vishnu's incarnations.

> This print entitled "Shiva and Parvati" shows them as husband and wife with the goddess Ganga issuing the River Ganges from Shiva's hair.

∧ This scene entitled "Shri Shesh Shaia" includes the multiheaded serpent who protects Vishnu in his sleep and the four-headed god Brahma springing from Vishnu's navel, thus creating our illusory world known as Maya. The painting is by L. N. Sharma for the Picture Publicity Company, Bombay.

^ Saraswati, the goddess of learning and knowledge, is widely
worshipped by students at the beginning of the school year.
This print is from a painting by S. M. Pandit.

∧ An early lithograph features the goddess Durga Mata
in schematic form as a trident with a third eye.

> A print published by Ravi Varma Press depicts
the powerful multiple-armed goddess Durga, who
was created by combining the best attributes of
powerful male gods in order to conquer the
"undefeatable" demon Mahishasura.

^ In this famous print from Ravi Varma Press, the goddess Kali sticks her tongue out to catch the dripping blood from the demon Raktabija in order to prevent his rejuvenation.

> Kali is also a patron goddess of Kolkata, the capital city of Bengal, and is shown here in a stylized form by Modern Litho Works, Bombay.

∧ Laxmi, the goddess of wealth, was born out
of the foam at the beginning of time.

‹ The goddess Laxmi is flanked by elephants showering
her with water, both symbols of abundance.

< During Diwali, the Festival of Light, lamps are lit to welcome Laxmi, the goddess of wealth. Here she is depicted in an advertisement for H. R. Laxmichand Gupta, selling ground nuts, oil, and sugar.

^ The theme of illumination also carried over to matchbook covers, as in these examples from the first half of the twentieth century.

DAMP PROOF

HIGH JUMP

SAFETY MATCHES

SOCIALISM

NIMCO

K.T.O.T. & SONS
NIMCO DINDIGUL

SAFETY MATCHES

झोर-भरत

PRICE Rs. 0-06

PRICE Rs. 0-03

ராம்நாட் மேச் இண்டஸ்ரீஸ்
தம்மநாயக்கன்பட்டி

M/s HASHMATRAI & SONS
SATTUR & NAGPUR.

KALI

THE ESAVI INDIA MATCH
FACTORY CALCUTTA

Politics, religion, and fanciful and domestic scenes were among the seemingly limitless range of images used to sell matches in the early years of the twentieth century.

^ A matchbox cover showing a man playing field hockey,
a popular game in India that predates cricket.

RANI

INDIA

PriceRe.0-0-9

TECKCHAND TILLUMAL
PILIBHIT.(U.P.)

LAKSHIMI

PRICE RE.0-0-6

சேமாதி பேசு ஸ்ரீ க்ஷ சாகதூர்

CHANDRA TRADERS, 36G
HALBADEVI RD.-BOMBAY

LOTUS LADY

PRICE
RE.0.0.6

COMORIN MATCH INDUSTRIES
(PRIVATE)LTD.KOVILPATTI

बेगम

INDIA

PRICE
RE.0-0-9
SAFETY MATCHES

KADIRIA MATCH FACTORY
KOVILPATTI.

∧ "Lotus Lady" and other beauties adorn these matchboxes,
which sold at the time for .06 and .09 rupees.

✔ Matchbook covers celebrating nationhood.

^ An image of an armed rebel woman from Karthigayan Matchworks.

∧ Matchbox covers featuring advertising
and images of modern transportation.

^ A fabric label entitled "Two Pals" from the New Jehangir Vakil Mills, Ltd., Bhavnagar.

< A stock 1930s advertising card shows a woman shopping in a Western-style shoe store. The store information has yet to be printed in the blank spaces.

^ Telephone Brand Sat-Isabgol, a nutritional supplement made with psyllium husk.

> An art deco-style fabric label portraying a woman pouring over letters.

> An old bottle of East Indian Condiments Brand Chutney, made by Merwanjee Poonjiajee & Sons, Bombay.

संतरा केश तेला

SANTRA HAIR OIL

روغن سنترہ

CHAMELI Oil चमेली ऑयल

Package labels for Santra, Chameli, and Dhania hair products.

^ Soap made with neem, a bitter herb associated with religious ceremonies.

For Dental Cleanliness
Ayurvedic Medicine

MONKEY
BRAND
BLACK
TOOTH POWDER

MANUFACTURED BY:
NOGI & CO. PVT. LTD.
SUREN ROAD, ANDHERI (E),
MUMBAI-400 093.

^ Monkey Brand Black Tooth Powder, manufactred by Nogi & Co., Mumbai.

> Image from the wrapper of Kesh Nikhar Hair Wash Soap, made in Haryana, India.

> A calendar for 1959 showing the many "Beauty Aids" sold by the E. S. Patanwala Company, Bombay.

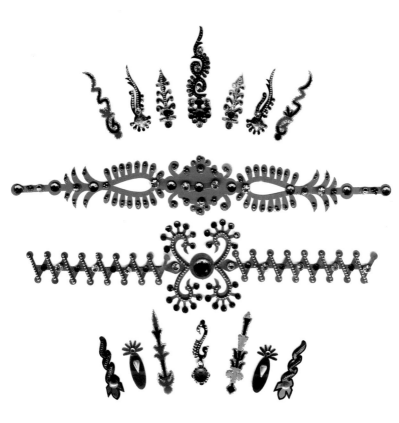

Decorative body ornaments called *bindi* are
worn by women to enhance their beauty on all
sorts of occasions. The bindis, left, are for the
eyebrows and the navel, the long ones, top, are
for the arms, and the singles, above, are for the
third-eye position on the forehead.

^ A shopping bag from the Chandnani Clothing Store,
selling fabric as well as ready-made clothing.

> Two bags advertising *paan masala* (chewing tobacco).
Opposite top is Sanjog brand and opposite bottom is Natkhat brand.

जिसने खाया, उसी ने अपनाया !
संजोग
पान मसाला
STATUTORY WARNING : CHEWING OF PAN MASALA MAY BE INJURIOUS TO HEALTH. NOT FOR MINORS.

नटखट™

^ A packet of "Unmanufactured" chewing tobacco, a cure
for constipation, from the Choubey Tambaku Factory,
Bhagalpur, north of Kolkata.

∧ A large tin of Scorpion Brand Snuff, from Jodhpur, Rajasthan.

Snuff is made from tobacco leaves scented with flavors
like menthol, camphor wood, and various types of flowers.

^ Clockwise from top left: Photo Brand Bhanwar Snuff, Baba Brand
Snuff, Rani Site Brand Snuff, and Kumar Brand Snuff.

∧ Little tins of Afghan
Khushdil Tobacco and
Raja Brand Snuff.

> A tin of Baby Brand
snuff.

∨ Packets of Seven
Photos Brand Snuff
and Raja Brand Snuff.

^ An Indian-style cigarette known as a *beedi* is a flavored and rolled tobacco leaf that has numerous regional manufacturers.

> "Real tobacco for enjoyment," states this Guarati-language tin sign for Taj Brand Tobacco.

અસ્સલ તંબાકુની
લહેજત માટે...
તાજ
છાપ
પીઓ
તાજ છાપ
TAJ BRAND
CIGARETTES
ઊતમ વરજીનીઆ
સીગારેટ
GTC
GOLDEN TOBACCO COMPANY PRIVATE LTD
ગોલ્ડન ટોબેકો કંપની પ્રાઈવેટ લિમીટેડ, મુંબઇ-૫૫
હિંદનો આ પ્રકારનો મોટામાં મોટો રાષ્ટ્રિય ઉદ્યોગ

^ A cloth banner advertises Khatri Brothers Snuff Shop in Rajasthan, the "land of many rajas."

^ An old tin sign pointing the way to a shop selling wheat flour and other groceries.

> A tin sign advertising lightbulbs.

^ Wrappers on boxes of Sugandha Shringar and
NR Vasu Special Ooda Bathi brand incense.

∧ Eagle Brand manufactures Gowlochan, tiny packets of processed cow dung that is mixed in water and used in purification ceremonies in the home.

> A tin of Bangla Darbar Batti stick incense, manufactured by Bhartiya Dhoop Karyalaya, Delhi.

Two government-sponsored brochures from the 1940s for train travel. Left, to Benares (now called Varanasi) on the sacred Ganges river and, right, to the resort and religious shrines of Mount Abu.

MOUNT ABU

BB & CIR

^ Statue of Bahubali at Shravanabelogoda, a famous pilgrimage site of the Jain religion. Nudity is a feature of Jainist iconography as a form of renunciation of worldly things.

INDIA

AGRA

> A brochure featuring the sights of Agra, home of the Taj Mahal, produced by the Ministry of Information and Broadcasting, Traffic Branch, Government of India.

119

MANIPURI DANCER *India*

⌃ A travel poster showing a type of classical dance from northeast India, printed by the Department of Tourism, 1959.

> A travel poster advertising the sights of Mount Abu in Rajasthan, issued by the Ministry of Transportation of India.

MOUNT ABU

VISIT INDIA

Luggage labels from
Mumbai, Kolkata,
and New Delhi.

Updated luggage label designs for the legendary Taj Mahal Hotel in Mumbai.

Two luggage labels
from hotels in New Dehli,
top, and two from Mysore State
(now called Karnataka), below.

< A promotional fan
for Air India from
the 1960s.

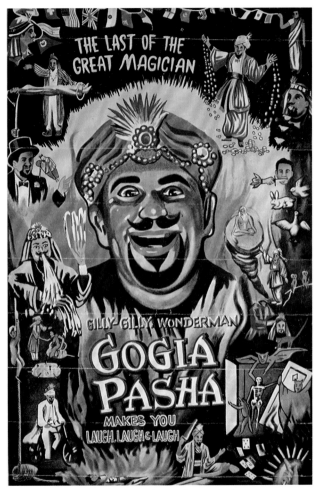

^ A poster for the "Gilly-Gilly Wonderman," Gogia Pasha,
a magician based in the town of Dehradun, 1956.

^ Day-Glo colors decorate this poster advertising the Asiad Circus.

^ A press photo for Mr. "Best-Built Parsi, 1960."

^ An early twentieth-century photo of an unknown wrestler,
by Rembrandt Studios, Bombay.

A poster entitled "Prabhu Gita" (Lord of Song) in which the famous song in praise of Lord Krishna, called "Jai Jagdish Hara," is interpreted as an elaborate dance performance. The poster names R. N. Bhargava of the devotional art school Bhargava Bhaktha Kala Niketan as the dancer in the photos.

131

^ A poster depicting the execution by the British of the
fifteen-year-old freedom fighter Khudiram in 1908, published
by Associated Calendars, Sivakasi.

> "Fighters of ancient times are giving them blessings! Hindustan's
brave young soldiers are fighting to save our house, property,
land, and valuables from the demonic enemy [Germany, Italy, and
Japan]," states this World War II era nationalistic poster.

शत्रूच्या तड्यापासून आमचें घरदार, जमीन जुमला व
मालमत्ता यांचें संरक्षण करण्यासाठीं हिंदुस्थानचे
शूर वीर राक्षसी शत्रूशीं लढत आहेत.

प्राचीनकालचे योद्धे त्यांना
आशीर्वाद देत आहेत.

^ A postage stamp from 1957, the one-hundreth-year anniversary of the Indian Mutiny.

^ A lithograph depicting the modern Indian republic's founding father, Mahatma Gandhi, printed by Ravi Varma Press, Malavli.

∧ This print showing scenes of industry sharing gears
with agriculture was painted by M. D. Singh.

^ A poster entitled "Great Indian Heros" declares "Hail to Mother India" and commemorates national figures, both ancient and modern, including, clockwise from top left, Shivaji, Rana Pratap, Subhas Chandra Bose, Chandra Shekhar Azad, and Shahid Bhagat Singh.

Toy cars made from recycled aluminum.

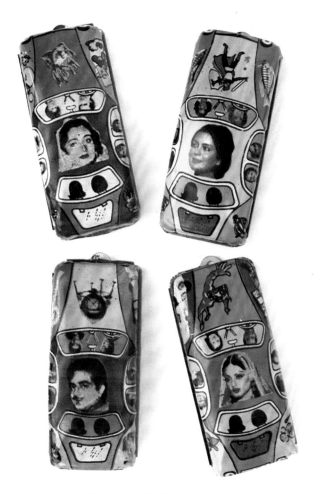

Toy cars with the faces of Bollywood stars on their roofs.

^ A page from an old vocabulary book of the Bengali language.

^ The Kamel Brand *Hindi Children's Book*
for learning the alphabet.

पी॰ एच॰ ई॰ डी॰ ने है ठाना,
घर – घर शौचालय बनवाना।

बिहार सरकार
लोक स्वास्थ्य अभियंत्रण विभाग
द्वारा जनहित में जारी

^ "Health for the people" states this public service postcard
announcing the goal of the Department of Tourism and Human
Resources of Bihar: a toilet for every household.

SRI RAM Madurai - 1. PHONE : 733982, 736731   NO. 60

∧ This is an example of a genre of affordable charts that became
very helpful to teachers in public schools, especially in poorer areas.
They not only taught vocabulary but also relayed Indian values and
customs to a whole generation of children.

Dr. B.K. AMBEDKAR

RAJIV GANDHI

M G RAMACHANDRAN

KAMBAR

RAJA RAJA CHOZAN

ELANGHO

∧ This is a detail from an educational chart showing some of India's noteworthy statesmen and religious leaders. Though the charts are often in English they are not necessarily used to teach the language.

> A chart entitled "Some Occasions" shows activities of interest to girls and was published by Mahesh Arts in India's capital of printing, Sivakasi.

SOME OCCASIONS

CRADLE CEREMONY

MARRIAGE FUNCTION

SCHOOL CAMP

TONSURE FUNCTION

GRAHA PRAVESH FUNCTION

BIRTH DAY PARTY

FAMILY PICNIC

ELECTRICAL APPLIANCES

TWO-IN-ONE (RADIO)

ELECTRIC IRON

ELECTRIC BELL

TELEPHONE

RADIO

ROOM COOLER

TABLE & CEILING FANS

TAPE RECORDER

TRANSISTOR

ELECTRIC SHAVER

ROOM HEATER

TELEVISION

REFRIGERATOR

ELECTRIC CLOCK

BREAD TOASTER

ELECTRIC KETTLE

ELECTRIC HEATER

WASHING MACHINE

COFFEE PERCOLATOR

GEYSER

MIXER (Mixi)

FLUORESCENT TUBE

TABLE LAMP

Sri Ram

^ A chart showing principles of the natural sciences entitled
"Sources of Water and Shadow," printed by Shri Ram in Madurai.

< A chart for learning the English names
for electrical appliances, by Shri Ram.

OCCUPATION

FARMER

GOLDSMITH

CARPENTER

BLACK SMITH

COBBLER

WASHER MAN

WEAWER

SCAVENGER

FISHER MAN

PRINTER

BARBER

MASON

TAILOR

VESSEL MAKER

TREECLIMBER

POTTER

42

Sri Ram Madurai

^ A chart showing the occupations of the working classes: craftsmen, tradesmen, and farmers.

> A detail from a chart showing the orderly world of "Municipal Committee Service."

Road & Street lights

Libraries

Water Supply

Fire Brigade

^ A chart called "Our Helpers" shows
occupations related to civic order and health.

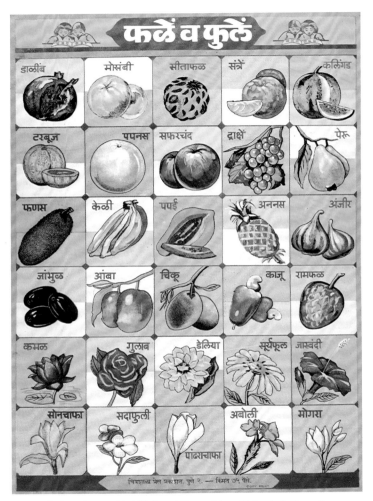

A vocabulary chart entitled "Fruit and Flowers" from Chitrashala Press, Poona.

तरी	जहाज	झझझर	
ठ ड	डलिया	ढ टकना	ण
य	द्वात द	ध धनुष	
फ	ब बतक	भ भगत	
र	ल लद्दू	व वजन	
स	ह		

^ An educational chart entitled "Anka Bodh" (Numbers Illustrated) from Chitrashala Press, Poona.

< Detail from an educational chart entitled "The Hindi Alphabet in Pictures" from Chitrashala Press, Poona.

श्री महा शिवरात्रि

Third Edition.

< A religious pamphlet entitled "Shree Maha Shivaratri" (In Praise of Lord Shiva), written by Puwipa, 1931.

બાલરામાયણ

> Lakshmana, Sita, and Rama go hunting in this book of stories entitled *The Ramayana for Children,* written in the Gujarati language, 1930s.

> A prayer book to be used during Vratotsav, a religious celebration, written by Purushotham Sharma Chaturvedi, 1961.

< A prayer book for *pooja* (worship) of the Shiva Linga by women, written in the Bengali language, 1960s.

155

^ A book about Indian theater entitled
Natrang by Nomichand Jain.

^ A book of poems entitled
Inner Bliss written in Urdu,
a language of northern India
and of Pakistan.

^ A book of poems written in
Bengali called *Another Kind
of Construction.*

^ A book entitled *The Rhythms of Bengali Poetry.*

^ A comic book entitled *My Uncle and the Magician Dakla*
by Diamond Comics, New Delhi.

∧ Comic book tales of horror and the supernatural, clockwise from top left:
Rama and Rahim and the Golden Tomb, Manoj Comics; *According to the Law*,
with Press Reporter Vashal, Durga Pocketbooks; *The Living Hand of a Corpse*,
Pawan Comics; and *The Murder on Video Cassette*, Tulsi Comics.

^ Comic books featuring heroic feats, clockwise from top left:
The Age of Demons, Tulsi Comics; *Flaming Anger*, Manoj Comics;
Azgar and The Lion King, Manoj Comics; and *The Tantric Priest
and the Goddess of Death*, Manoj Comics.

^ A comic book entitled *Haunted Palace* from Manoj Comics, Delhi.

^ Wooden statue of the ten headed villain Ruvana
from the epic story Ramayana.

> A selection of eyes of gods and goddesses from a store in
Rajasthan that specializes in replacement eyes for all sizes of
statues of human deities, as well as eyes for elephant and cow gods.

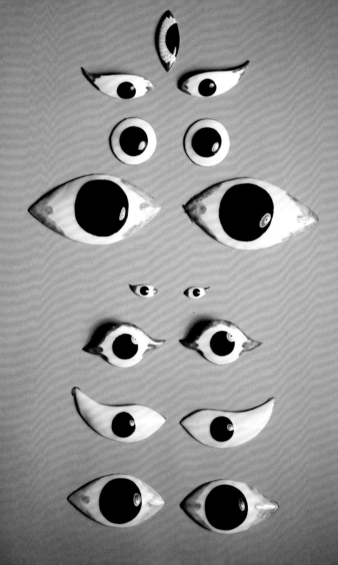

^ A papier-mâché mask of Lord Jagannath.

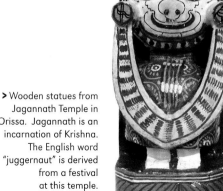

> Wooden statues from
Jagannath Temple in
Orissa. Jagannath is an
incarnation of Krishna.
The English word
"juggernaut" is derived
from a festival
at this temple.

बुरी नज़र वाले तेरा मुँह काला

Tin plaques of a deity who turns away the evil eye are
to be hung above main entrances to shops and homes.

^ A version of a royal turban called a *kirita* to be worn at festivities.

^ Colorfully designed envelopes for offering money
as a gift at weddings and other occasions.

Standard

CAKE
BOMBS
ORDINARY

THE STANDARD FIREWORKS INDUSTRIES, SIVAKASI.

India is second only to China in the size of its fireworks industry (largely because of the role fireworks play in religious ceremonies) and has developed a distinctly Indian style of label art. Here young women are startled by Standard brand firecrackers called "Cake Bombs" and "Mine of Serpents."

The Standard Fireworks brand, from the southern city of Sivakasi, dominates the Indian fireworks industry and is noteworthy for its topical labels.

^ "Made without child labour" states this cloth shop banner for the Anil Fancy Fireworks Factory.

> Almost all fireworks in India are produced in the southern city of Sivakasi because of its dry climate, long-established printing industry, and nearby useful minerals.

SIVAKASI - 626 123.

> A package of Peacock Crackers gives an Indian theme to a Chinese-style label.

^ The Red Fort, a national monument in Delhi, appears on this firecracker called "Flash Thunder."

ANIL

EMERALD

website: www.anilgroup.com

ANIL FIREWORKS FACTORY, SOORARPATTI.

< Fireworks are an important part of the Ganapati festival, which honors the elephant-headed god Ganesh.

177

Fireworks explode day and night during the festival of Diwali in order to drive out Alakmi, the goddess of bad luck.

"Is he a revolutionary? Is he a helper? Is he a thief? Take your pick then find your answer by seeing the movie!" states this flyer for the movie *Bagi* (The Rebel), directed by Dhirubhai Desai. Brochures as promotion and as souvenirs were a large part of the movie-going experience in India. These two striking designs are part of one flyer.

VISHNU present

वंडखोर बाग़ी

BAGI

DIRECTOR:- DHIRUBHAI DESAI.

^ "Spring time is love time" states this ad for the movie *Bahar* (The Spring), which ran in the magazine *Filmindia* in October 1951.

^ A brochure cover for an action-adventure film called *Paras Mani* (The Touchstone) directed by Babubhai Mistry, 1963.

Shorey Films

PRESENTS

MEENA

IN

EK
DO
TEEN

WITH

MOTILAL

MAJNU · YASHODHRA KATJU

AND **KAUSHALYA**

एक दो तीन

Pamart

ایک دو تین

Produced & Directecd by

ROOP K. SHOREY

∧ *Vanraj, the Jangle King* [*sic*], starring
John Cawas and Krishna Kumari, 1952.

< A movie entitled *Ek Do Teen* (One Two Three),
starring the young 1950s celebrity starlet Meena.

^ An early Bollywood poster for the movie *Atom Bomb*,
made in the 1940s by Basant Pictures, which was known
at the time for making mass-market "stunt films."

> *Talwar Ka Dhani* (The Sound of the Sword), a Hindi-language
swashbuckler starring Nadira, filmed in 1956 by Vikas Productions.

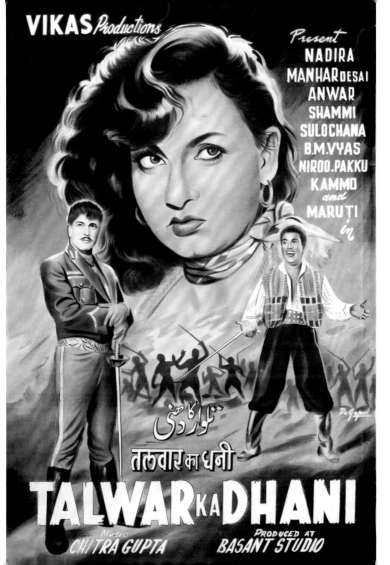

REGD NO B.3517
filmindia
OCTOBER - 1951
INLAND RS. 3/-
FOREIGN SH. 6/-
Suraiya
IN
KULDIP SEHGAL'S
JALWA
Directed by
ANANT THAKUR
A KULDIP PICTURES LTD. PRODUCTIO
M/S. KULDIP PICTURES LTD.
SARITA VILLA

^ A *Filmindia* magazine cover for October 1951 featuring actress and singer Suraiya in a movie called *Jalwa* (Feature).

< An advertisement for the film *Jalpari* (Water Nymph), starring Ashok Kumar and Nalini Jaywan, 1951.

^ The cover of *Filmindia* magazine for June 1948 featured the
film *Ghungroo* (Ankle Bells) and was published in Bombay,
the center of the film industry.

> A calendar portrait of the actress Sadna, from the 1960s.

^ In this movie, *Hari Darshan* (Holy Worship), the evil Lord Ravan threatens the worshippers of Bhagwan Vishnu with death, but their piety prevails.

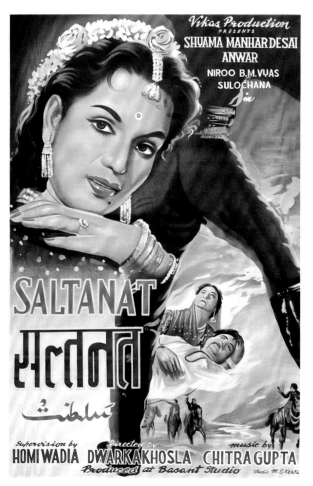

^ Shyama Manhardesai stars in *Saltanat* (Sultan's Woman),
a movie supervised by Homi Wadia, whose work goes back
to the earliest days of Indian movies.

^ Film prince Ashok Kumar reigned in Bollywood from the 1930s to 1960s. His film *Kismet* broke a record as the highest-earning film in 1943.

‹ A calendar photo of a midcentury Bollywood beauty.

যারে বেলুন মায়ের কাছে
খোকন বড় কষ্টে আছে

ব.শ্যামা পিক্চার্সের
বন্দী বলাকা

অপর্ণা · দীপঙ্কর
সুমিত্রা · গীতা দে
অনামিকা · সত বসু
মা. বুবু

প্রযোজনা—হেমা চ্যাটার্জী   পরিচালনা—ইন্দর সেন সুর শ্যামল মিত্র পরিবেশনা চণ্ডীমাতা ফি

∧ A poster for the movie *Alakh Niranjan* (One's True Self), which had action, romance, mythological themes, and a pet feline, 1975.

< A poster for a Bengali film entitled *Bandi Balaka*
(The Imprisoned Crane) states "Go on, balloon, to find mother."

बच्चे मन के स...
सारे जग...
आँख के त...
ये वो नन्हे फूल...
जो भगवान...
लगते प्...

^ A poster for the movie *Do Kaliyan* (Two Rose Buds), the story of two girls "that everyone adores," directed by Krishnanpanju.

> *Ghunghat* (The Veil), a social drama from the 1960s.

GHUNGHAT

a GEMINI PICTURE

घूंघट

जेमिनी
चित्र

^ A film leaflet for the movie *Patanga* (Small Bees), 1971.

> An advertisement for *Umang* (Enthusiasm), "a dynamic film about modern youth," from 1971.

^ A movie entitled *Albeli,* 1951, starred screen-queen Geeta Bali as the title character and who was nominated for best actress by the Filmfare Awards for a later film *Vachan* (Promise), in 1955.

भाग्यलक्ष्मी चित्रमन्दिर कृत

जय संतोषी माँ
JAI SANTOSHI MAA

∧ This movie entitled *Jai Santoshi Maa* (Hail to Mother Santoshi), 1975, elevated Santoshi Maa, a minor regional deity known as the goddess of satisfaction, into the Hindu pantheon throughout the country. Bollywood's power is also such that it has propelled many actors into political office.

< The "lovely" superstar Hema Malini, right, as a nymph descended from heaven in the Hindu musical epic *Hare Krishna*, which the poster states was "endorsed by the Chief Minister of Madras."

203

दास्ताने लैला मजनूँ

S.G. LAAD PRESENTS
CHANDRA ART'S
dastan-e
Laila
Majnu

داستان ليلى مجنون

PRODUCED & DIRECTED BY
R.L. DESAI
MUSIC
IQBAL QURESHI
LYRICS
JANISAR AKHTAR
CO PRODUCERS
JAIDEO-RAMZAN BIKANERI
SCREEN PLAY & DIALOGUES   PHOTOGRAPHY
ZAFAR RAHI · A. DESAI

EASTMANCOLOR

^ Bollywood's queen of tragedy, Meena Kumari, stars in *Kaajal* (Eyeliner), 1965.

< A poster for *Laila and Majnu*, an Indian version of the Romeo and Juliet story.

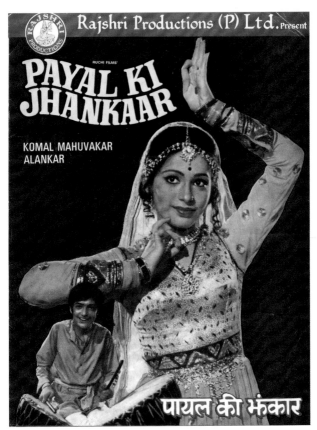

Rajshri Productions (P) Ltd. Present

RUCHI FILMS'

PAYAL KI JHANKAAR

KOMAL MAHUVAKAR
ALANKAR

पायल की झंकार

^ A booklet for the film *Payal Ki Jhankaar* (The Tinkling
of Anklets), a Bollywood musical made in 1980.

> *Gaai Aur Gori* (A Cow and a Girl) was a romantic
film directed by M. A. Thirumugam in 1973.

DEVAR PRESENTS

DHANDAYUTHAPANI FILMS

Gaai aur Gori

EASTMAN COLOUR... BY GEMINI

गाय और गोरी

گائے اور گوری

EDITING - DIRECTION
M.A.THIRUMUGAM

MUSIC
LAXMIKANT PYARELAL

STORY & PRODUCED BY
SANDOW M.M.A.CHINNAPPA DEVAR

Both the LP cover, above, and the movie poster, right, show the energetic singing and dancing that made the film *Sargam* (Musical Notes), starring Rishi Kapoor, a Bollywood blockbuster musical in 1979. The song "Dafiwale" was one of the biggest songs of that year.

MANMOHAN DESAI'S

ALLAH-RAKHA

PRODUCED & DIRECTED BY
KETAN DESAI

अल्लाररखा

< *Allah Rakha*
(Belong to God)
was made in
1976.

> *Dushman
Devta* (The
Enemy and God)
produced by
the prominent
filmmaker Anil
Ganguly in 1991.

MUSIC   STORY   SCREENPLAY   EXECUTIVE PRODUCER

∧ A flyer for the movie *Nache Mayuri* (The Dancing Peacock).

> *Chandni*, starring Do Anjaane as the title character, was produced in 1979 by Yash Chopra, winner of the Filmfare Award, the oldest film award in India.

^ Clockwise from top left: Records of songs from the films *Rungoli* (Colors), *Do Raaste* (Cross Road), *Diwana* (The Lovestruck Man), and *Sadhna*.

< A publicity photo for a glamorous screen queen.

JIS DESH MEN GANGA BEHTI HAI

ANGEL RECORDS

∧ The soundtrack record for *Jis Desh Men Ganga Behti Hai*
(The Land Where the Ganga Flows) starred popular actor Raj Kapoor.

< Album covers for the soundtracks of the romance dramas
Sadma (A Surprise) and *Shabab* (The Beauty).

Four musical
soundtrack records
from popular movies
in the Tamil language
of southern India.
For a time in the
1960s, Tamil-language
movies were second
only to those in Hindi
in popularity.

> Music from the
movies *Sun Rising
from the West*,
top, and *So
Precious*, bottom.

◀ Music from two Tamil movies starring the superstar actor and politician M. G. Ramachandran: *One Mother's Sons*, top, and *Spring Mansion*, bottom.

220

More and more people choose

BEDROCK B
SCOOTER, MOPED, CYCLE & CYCLE
RICKSHAW TUBES

INTERNATIONAL
SCOOTER, MOPED, CYCLE & CYCLE
RICKSHAW TYRES

Manufactured by
International Rubber & Gen. Inds P. Ltd. Bombay
Bedrock Tyre & Rubber Company, Bombay

DEALERS :

VENKATESHWARA & CO.

CYCLE PARTS
BUS STAND, NIRMAL, (DIST. ADILABAD).

⌃ Many calenders that depicted sacred figures and sites ended up in the household altar. Here is Ganesh, the god for destroying obstacles and a popular image to start a new year, on a calendar advertising a store selling "cycle parts."

< A dancing Krishna on a Burmah Shell Oil Company calendar from 1939.

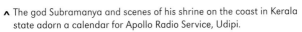

^ The god Subramanya and scenes of his shrine on the coast in Kerala state adorn a calendar for Apollo Radio Service, Udipi.

∧ A print of an idealized bride in a red sari for Fancy
  Shoes Mart and Janta Boot House, Karnataka.

Two calendar beauties posing against backdrops of idealized agricultural and industrial progress. The actress above, Saira Banu, was a teen favorite who starred in a hit movie called *Junglee* (Jungle), in 1961.

H.R.Roja.

^ A calendar image of a saleswoman displaying colorful bolts of fabric for saris.

^ A calendar depicting a woman serving tea in a stylish home.

^ A stock calendar image of childhood
ready for advertising to be printed on it.

> A beauty with a candle on a promotional calendar for "Lovely
Electric and Photo Store" located in Sadar Bazaar, Guna.

SREE PRABHAKARA STORES
ಶ್ರೀ ಪ್ರಭಾಕರ ಸ್ಟೋರ್ಸ್, ಗುಂಡೋಪಂತರ ಬೀದಿ, ಬೆಂಗಳೂರು-೨

Khara Dall, Green Dall, Beedi & Cigarettes & Banana
Raja Rathnam Market, G. P. Street,
BANGALORE-2

^ Vanisree was a versatile screen star who appeared in a non-Bollywood film genre called Kollywood (so named because the films were made in the Kodambakkam region of Tamil Nadu). She also appeared in films speaking Telugu, Kannada, and Malayalam. This calendar, for 1974, advertises a shop in Bangalore.

^ A woman applies *kaajal*, a traditional eyeliner, on this calendar image for 1977.

ANANT RAM GUPTA

DEALERS IN : QUALITY CALENDARS, PICTURES & WEDDING CARDS

Shop : 4094, NAI SARAK, DELHI-110 006

Office : 2572, **CHAWRI BAZAR, DELHI-110 006**

∧ The proliferation of calendars displaying religious themes accelerated the evolution of devotional art styles in the latter half of the twentieth century. Here Hanuman, the monkey god, leads Rama and Laxmana over dangerous waters, on a calendar from a manufacturer of "quality calendars, pictures & wedding cards" in Delhi.

^ The painting *Shiva*, by S.M. Pandit, shows a trend in
heightened realism in devotional prints and also shows
the influence of a cinemagraphic or "filmie" style.

∧ This print depicting the loving couple Vishnu and Laxmi breaks with traditional style and color and was printed by the Picture Publicity Company for Studio Meghani.

> This poster of Vishnu surrounded by his ten incarnations is in a transitional midcentury style.

The goddess of learning and knowledge, Saraswati,
is popular with students. She's also a patron goddess of art
and literature. These two versions of her show a progression
in the style of her representation. The version on the right
may have been modeled after Bollywood star Hema Malini.

∧ A modern approach to the innocence of children is reflected in these 1970s scenes from the god Krishna's childhood. Above, a young Krishna defeats Kaliya, the serpent king, by dancing continuously on top of him.

< Top, Baby Krishna is in the arms of his foster mother, Yashoda, and below, Baby Krishna has gotten into the butter again.

∧ Vivid colors distinguish this portrait of the tenth Sikh Guru, Govinh Singh, painted by Mohinder Singh. Sikhism is the fifth largest religion in the world.

‹ Hanuman, the monkey god, with the word "Ram" covering his body as a mantra indicating loyalty to the god Rama.

241

∧ Randal Maa, the daughter of Vishwakarma (the god of architecture), manifests herself as two beings — Sandhya and Chhaya — in order to save the earth from draught.

> The goddess Chamunda is represented as a vase on a golden lion throne with celestial attendants. By manipulating the printing process, contemporary publishers have created a poster genre of supersaturated colors.

^ Contemporary Hindu devotional pamphlets containing "Vrita Katha,"
or holy stories, including the story of Satyanarayama, Santoshi Matha,
Hanuman, and, lower right, stories for Wednesday fasting days.

^ A poster showing a popular pilgrimage site in Kerala called Subramanya, after the son of Shiva. The mantra above states, "When I am there why do you have fear?"

< The god Vishwakarma, architect of the world, is shown here with the implements of livelihood, on a poster for "Ayudha Pooja" or the blessing of tools.

^ All the gods and goddesses of all things, as well as the
Hindu trinity – Brahman, Vishnu, and Shiva – are contained
in this image of the sacred cow known as Kamadhenu.

∧ The title of this poster, "Ashirvad" (Blessings), refers to the many
auspicious symbols of palm reading that surround Lord Shiva.

In a country where religious observance is an integral part of everyday life, an expanding consumer culture offers many new forms of devotional items.

< A wooden statue of Brahma, one of the trinity of Hindu gods.

< A plastic statue of the adored Ganesh.

∧ A bobble-head Hindu priest character named Baba Ji made from clay.

> This electric Shiva made of plastic bejeweled with flashing colored lights updates a long tradition of decorated shrines.

Because of his approachable and beneficent nature, the beloved god Ganesh has become a playful subject for calendar artists.

^ A stand-up figure of the sacred cow, from a wedding supply store.

Acknowledgments

Kalim Winata wishes to thank all the wonderful friends that have helped make this book happen. In India, a special thanks goes to Aditya for his resoucefulness, Hemant for his invaluable conversations about Indian imagery, and the Khatri Brothers for the wonderful banner. In the United States, thanks go to John Stucky at the Asian Art Museum in San Francisco for his database-like memory, and Ronman for his friendship.

Reed Darmon wishes to thank Ravi Nayar for his translations, invaluable cultural insight, and friendship, and Steve Mockus at Chronicle Books for his trust and enthusiasm.

^ A matchbox cover advertising Stanes Baby Brand Tea Dust.

NEXT PAGE: Laxmi, the goddess of wealth, by Ravi Varma Press.